Monographic Journals of the Near East   *SMS* 3/4 (August 1980)

Terqa Preliminary Reports, No. 11
SOURCING TECHNIQUES FOR CERAMICS AND SOILS
AT TERQA AND RELATED SITES·

Nicholas M. Magalousis
Department of Anthropology
Chapman College

and

Institute of Archaeology
University of California, Los Angeles

Arthur Flint
Department of Geology
Chapman College

Vance Gritton
Department of Chemistry
Chapman College

George E. Miller
Department of Chemistry
University of California, Irvine

The primary objectives of this research were to (1) establish an overall orientation and framework for future analysis of this type at Terqa and (2) to determine on a preliminary basis the relationship of ceramics and soils of two sites in the Near East: ancient Terqa (modern Ashara in Syria) and Dilbat (modern Tell Deylem in Iraq). The long-term objective of this sourcing was to contribute data toward the reconstruction of social, political and economic trends.

A truly interdisciplinary effort was required, as several universities and analytical techniques were utilized—atomic absorption, optical emission, thin section, botanical and computer analyses. A general attempt was made to suggest and formulate a continuum of research standards, from the original field collection of samples to the actual laboratory analysis; this standardization would establish an overall climate of reproducibility and credibility.

The most important substantive results are found in the areas of ceramic composition, ceramic clay/soil relationships, atomic absorption and computer refinement for archaeological analysis.

· Sincere appreciation is extended to Dr. Giorgio Buccellati and Dr. Marilyn Kelly-Buccellati, Directors of the Joint American Expedition to Terqa; Dr. Clement Meighan, Department of Anthropology, Dr. Julius Glater, Department of Energy and Kinetics, Dr. I. Kaplan and Dr. E. Kalil, Department of Geophysics and Space Science, Mr. Dollase, Mr. R. Alkaly, Mr. N. Kettering, Department of Geology of the University of California at Los Angeles;—Dr. Frederick Kakis, Department of Organic Chemistry, Dr. Theodore Mortenson, Department of Botany, Mr. Andrew Barrett, Department of Physics, Mr. F. Price, Department of Art, Mr. Michael Weil, Department of Chemistry, and Miss Sidney West, Department of Computer Science, of Chapman College;—Dr. R. I. Frank, Department of History, University of California at Irvine;—Dr. Patricia Masters, Scripps Institute of Oceanography, Mrs. Fran Muir, Administrative Assistant, Interdisciplinary Research, Laguna Beach, California; Mr. Charles Ralph, Multimedia Productions, Santa Ana, California; and Dr. Donald C. Bradford, Finnigan Instrumentation, San Jose, California. This publication of the Joint Expedition to Terqa relates to materials excavated in the Fall of 1976, during the second season, which was made possible through a grant from the Samuel H. Kress Foundation and the Ambassador International Cultural Foundation.

TABLE OF CONTENTS

1. INTRODUCTION

N. M. Magalousis

1.1. Methodological Considerations

The trend toward specialization in the social sciences has resulted in a clearer definition of techniques and methods. At the same time, it has created an insular effect which has isolated disciplines from one another and even subgroups within each specific discipline. A more conscious effort has been made in recent years by several disciplines to merge their efforts and specialties in attempts to solve problems on a higher level of analysis. Archaeology is one area experiencing major interdisciplinary impacts as the need for a growing dependency on the physical sciences becomes more apparent. The expertise of physics, chemistry, soil science, geology and computer science has created new capabilities and possibilities with regard to the basic goal of historic and archaeological reconstruction.

The most dramatic examples thus far are found in the areas of radiocarbon dating, amino acid racemization, thermoluminescence, neutron activation and atomic absorption analysis. These varied techniques have the capabilities of determining the origins of traded items (sourcing) such as obsidian and ceramics, as well as placing artifactual data into a temporal chronology. Sourcing by neutron activation or atomic absorption analysis, for example, attempts to determine chemical element content of artifacts. This data is then related to geologic data in an attempt to determine ancient sources of clays, soils, lithics and minerals used in the manufacture of material goods.

Interdisciplinary cooperation is required in endeavors of this nature, although it may not be obvious that interdisciplinary connections exist between disciplines and may be beneficial to all concerned. When analytical interconnections are recognized, it is then sometimes difficult to communicate various internal disciplinary problems to the other disciplines; for example, field or technical practices that may alter analytical results such as the altering of chemical element content in the artifactual assemblage.

In an interpretive sense, one may ask if an analytical and interpretive continuum can realistically become attainable if all the variables are considered. There may, in fact, never be the means for achieving a complete retrieval of man's past relating to the elusive elements of social, political, economic and other intricacies. Nevertheless, our overall percentage error can be dramatically reduced and our accuracy relating to historic and archaeological reconstruction can be significantly increased. The approach to a more reliable and accurate analytical and interpretive framework is clear. As in other cases, it is always the first steps which are difficult to operationalize. Once established, the framework will be self-supportive and self-perpetuating as the interlocking paradigms become clear to archaeology, more internal standardization and communication will be established, thus maintaining an environment where a high degree of reproducibility exists.

1.2. Technical Considerations

Specifically concerning archaeology and the elemental analysis of artifacts, the following variables should be seriously considered if a continuum is to be established from the excavation to the laboratory: sampling techniques, standardization of recording, factors of contamination, temperatures, and analytical instrumentation.

Geology. (1) Complete geologic profiles should be compiled for all archaeological regions of interest. (2) Macro- and trace element "fingerprints" should be determined for each geologic and geographic region of interest; this data may then be compared to the artifactual assemblage. (3) Ancient clay sources should be determined for each geologic and cultural region. In addition, attention should be paid to nontransportable clay/ceramic materials such as brick from stratified structures. These nontransportable or nontrade materials may at times serve as a benchmark for fingerprinting and isolating macro- and rare-earth elements. In conjunction with element analysis, thin-section analysis may be employed to enlarge the data base, which would lend more credibility and dependability to theoretical assumptions regarding trade patterns. (4) Whenever possible, it would be advantageous to identify the aforementioned ancient clay sources and determine if, or in what way, the clay sources have been altered by environmental conditions after hundreds or thousands of years. Additional consideration should be made to determine whether or not clays were at any time traded intra- or interculturally for some specialized reason, such as religion or pigmentation.

Contamination and Inclusions. (1) Buried in the soil, artifacts may change through time. For example, ceramic artifacts contain small voids; these voids, through the presence of moisture and natural or unnatural drainage of the soil, may accumulate or deposit foreign materials that may ultimately be reflected in chemical results. (2) The effect of temper inclusions on analytical results is also of major importance, in that the ancient potter may have introduced impurities to make original clay conform to standards or needs. This is sometimes accomplished by inclusions of sand or shell. (3) The effects of slip, temper, paint and glaze on element analysis must also be resolved in the laboratory sampling technique. This problem does not seem to apply to most early Mesopotamian ceramics, as little slip or paint was used. (4) Firing temperatures may also alter or mask element content in some way.

Formal Corpora. Defined artifactual corpora must also be prepared for each cultural area, including variant artifacts. Corpora should include such information as the object's form, function, fabric, Munsell color values and a detailed photograph. This will facilitate rapid identification and comparison of artifactual types (Refer to Appendix II).

Standardization of Procedures. Standardization of sample preparation and the analytical process begins at the archaeological excavation as the archaeologist removes the object from the soil with his trowel. From this point forward a variety of contamination factors may be introduced: by attempting to clean artifacts in solutions such as river water and acids, by general handling, and by packaging of artifacts to be sent from the field to the laboratory. As noted previously, a continuum of standards should be accomplished governing even this area of analysis.

1.3. Substantive Considerations:
Terqa and Dilbat

This research endeavor is preliminary in nature, as the assemblage of artifacts is based on the second season of excavation at Terqa and surrounding area (see *TPR 1* for a general description of the site), and from a surface collection from Dilbat in Iraq. On a long-term basis, it is expected that this form of analysis will establish a large and interrelated data base and data bank. This base will include formal corpora related to archaeology, history, geology and chemistry.

During the second season of excavation, no particular sampling techniques were used in the collection of this data. In the future, this data will be compared to formal corpora data and the overall stratified site data. From Dilbat, ceramic samples were selected for diagnostic traits during visits to the site in 1971 and 1976 (G. Buccellati and M. Kelly-Buccellati will report separately on their survey for the site).

Provided below is a general inventory of the archaeological assemblage used for this research.

1.3.1. Soils and Clays

A.   **Soils and clays** taken from Terqa, MP2, MP4, MP5, MP6, SG3, SG4 (stratified and unstratified samples)
B.   **Soils and clays** taken from the opposite bank of the Euphrates from Terqa
C.   **Soils and clays** taken from the hills to the west of Terqa, all within a radius of 35 kms. from Terqa
D.   **Soils and clays** taken from the Mari and Baghouz areas
E.   **Clays** used by modern potters at a ceramic manufacturing company near Terqa

1.3.2. Ceramics

A.   **Ceramics** were analyzed from Terqa, Mari and Dilbat (stratified and unstratified)
B.   **Brick** samples from Terqa

A total of 194 samples are represented in this study.

2. A PRELIMINARY THIN-SECTION ANALYSIS OF
TERQA AND DILBAT CERAMICS

A. Flint

2.1. Introduction

This part of the investigation employed the petrographic polarizing microscope to study thin sections of ceramic artifacts recovered from Terqa and Dilbat. The standard technique requires sections of the ceramic to be abraded to a thickness of 0.03 mm., and cemented to a microscope slide with a cement of known index of refraction. Thus prepared, the thin section, as it is called, is ready for study under the polarizing microscope at magnifications of from 40X to 400X, using transmitted light.

This approach to the study of ceramics permits (1) observation of the characteristics of the paste and temper, (2) the identification of the minerals and rock fragments that compose the temper, (3) an estimate of the relative amounts of each, and (4) a view of the amount, shape, and size of voids that are regularly present in the specimens.

The purpose of this part of the larger investigation is to learn if the similarities and differences observed by this standard petrographic procedure have value in (1) discerning different techniques employed in the manufacture of ceramics, (2) identifying ceramics manufactured in different geographic regions at different times, (3) identifying the different raw materials used, or (4) classifying ceramics according to these and other observed features.

The research focused on four aspects of the ceramic fragments:
    A.   The size, amount, and type of minerals composing the temper.
    B.   The amount of and structures in the paste.
    C.   The amount, size, shape, and orientation of voids in the ceramics.
    D.   Gross color of specimens and other features such as the presence or absence of slip.

2.2. Technical Analysis

2.2.1. Preliminary Summary of Terqa Thin Section Samples

A study of 46 thin sections prepared from ceramic shards from Terqa revealed the following preliminary data.

Temper. Minerals composing the temper in the Terqa specimens consist mostly of quartz, orthoclase and plagioclase, with lesser amounts of other transparent minerals including augite, hornblende and some unidentified small secondary minerals. Opaque minerals, probably those of iron mostly, compose generally 3 to 4 percent of the thin section. Temper fragments range in size from near silt size to as much as 1.0 mm. in maximum diameter, and these are generally angular and consist of individual minerals, although a few rock fragments are also present. A number of sections contain as little as 2 percent transparent temper minerals, whereas others have more than 22 to 23 percent of these minerals (Samples T-28 and T-43). Most were less than 10 percent of the specimen. In many of the Terqa sections, a progressive change in the grain size of the transparent temper fragments from larger to smaller size fraction makes it difficult to distinguish which is temper and which is paste (Samples T-28 and T-43).

Except for the difference in the amount of temper, there seemed to be little to distinguish one section from another. Two specimens are distinctly different, however. Their temper includes relatively large (1.0 mm. or more in diameter) rounded grains of olivine or augite, intergrown with lath-shaped plagioclase minerals. These ceramics (Samples T-22 and T-45) were manufactured from a distinctly different raw material than any of the other slides.

Paste. The most distinctive feature of the paste in the Terqa fragments is that of color, which ranges from a light olive green to a deep red-brown. Between these two extremes are reddish-gray and reddish-brown hues, the amount of oxidized iron apparently giving a weak to strong reddish cast to the specimens. As noted above, the paste consists of clay and silt-size material grading without a perceptible break into the temper. For purposes of percentage composition, fragments about 0.08 mm. or larger are considered temper.

The paste is essentially structureless. No evidence that it ever was plastic or that it preferentially yielded to pressure during manufacture was observed in the thin sections.

Voids. One of two thin sections are estimated to have 45 to 50 percent of the total specimen in voids or holes (Samples T-10 and T-14). A few sections fall in the range of 30 to 45 percent void space, but the bulk of the sections show from 10 to 23 percent voids. A few specimens have very little in the way of holes. Where the voids represent a large part of the specimen, they are characteristically elongate and slender and are generally parallel to subparallel. In the specimens with less than 10 percent voids, the open spaces are commonly rounded in outline.

Slip. A darker rim, commonly discontinuous, is present in some slides in thicknesses of from 0.3 to 0.7 mm. (Samples T-37 and T-44). It does not appear to be slip, and seems more probably to be related to the ceramic firing process. No other suggestion of the application of any kind of slip to the ceramics was observed.

Other. In one specimen (Sample T-29) a long thin structure, thought possibly to be organic in origin, was noted.

2.2.2. Brick Specimens from Terqa

Thin sections of four brick specimens, designated A, B, C, and D, were examined, and significant differences were observed.

Temper in the specimens differed considerably in size of fragment. In specimens A and B the mineral fragments are fine, only a very few being larger than 0.1 mm. in diameter, and the fragments grade into the paste without a size break. In specimen C the fragments are significantly coarser than in A and B, and the paste is very fine grained. In specimen D most of the temper mineral fragments are relatively coarse, having diameters as much as 0.3 mm. and most are larger than 0.1 mm. Specimens C and D have a greater variety of minerals than either A and B or the ceramic specimens studied.

The **paste** in specimens A and B is very fine grained and composes most of the area of the brick in the section. There is relatively much less paste in specimens C and D, and in both the paste is somewhat coarser than in A and B. All the specimens contain rounded brown siltstone fragments to a maximum diameter of more than 2.2 mm. These larger rounded granules stand out sharply in contrast to the mineral fragments of the temper, which are consistently angular in outline.

Voids in the four specimens ranged from 15 to 40 percent of the total area of the thin section. In specimens A and B most of the voids were ameboid in shape, but in specimens C and D many of the voids had been occupied by long slender fibers, perhaps fine straw, which had decayed and disappeared in the specimens. Specimen C had an unusual abundance of voids attributed to the organic fibers.

A poor thin section of specimen B suggests that the brick was poorly cemented and friable, hence did not hold together well during grinding.

Both specimens C and D have dark splotchy areas that probably are manganese staining or carbon from smoke.

Sparse gypsum cement is present in specimen D, the only place where any was observed in the brick thin sections.

The abundance of organic fiber presumably used as a binder in specimens C and D, and the varying size and amount of the temper mineral fragments were the chief differences noted in these four specimens. Additional study may show these properties to be diagnostic in distinguishing bricks of different time periods.

2.2.3. Preliminary Summary of Dilbat Thin Section Samples

A study of 33 thin sections of Dilbat ceramic fragments provided the following preliminary observations.

Temper. The temper is composed of both opaque and transparent minerals. The opaques are commonly the minerals magnetite, some of which was oxidized to hematite before the specimen was sectioned, and ilmenite, an iron-titanium oxide. Opaque minerals range in amount from 1 to 10 percent of the total specimen (as viewed in the thin section) and in the average slide is 2 to 3 percent.

Most of the transparent minerals consisted of quartz, orthoclase and plagioclase, with quartz predominating. Other relatively high birefrigent minerals—augite, olivine, and possibly calcite—are less common in the specimens. Few thin sections contain temper in amounts greater than 10 percent of the specimen. Some sections show a considerable amount of red iron staining, assumed to have derived from the oxidation of magnetite. The iron staining gives a more-or-less reddish cast to most of the slides.

Paste. The paste is fine-grained, generally less than 0.08 mm. in size of individual fragments, and commonly lacking in structure, particularly any evidence of "flow" or yielding in the plastic state by pressures applied during manufacture. About six shades of color of the paste are recognized. These range from olive green, probably the basic original color, through shades of reddish brown, reddish gray-brown, to nearly black. Some black mottling, caused by concentrations of small black specks, is present in a number of slides (Sample D-3-5). This may reflect composition, possibly manganese, or may have been caused by the firing or baking process. In general, the differences in color seem not to be important in distinguishing the source of ancient ceramics, but this is not as yet clearly established.

Voids. Voids in the ceramics range from 20 to 50 percent of the total specimen (as viewed in the thin section). Larger voids—1.2 to 2 mm. in maximum dimension—tend to be elongate, and these are regularly oriented parallel or subparallel in the slides. Small voids, on the other hand, tend to be round to sub-round in outline (Sample D-2-10). One or two voids observed seemed to have crystals growing in the open space, but it is likely that these are temper fragments which formed a part of the wall of the void. Many of the voids are partly or entirely filled with fine pulverant crystalline debris from the grinding of the sections (Samples D-2-10 and D-11-3).

Slip. One or two specimens seem to have a thin slip at the edge as much as 3 mm. thick (Sample D-3-5). Most did not show even a suggestion of the presence of slip, but some show discontinuous borders of a darker hue thought, however, to have been related to the firing of the ceramics.

In the specimens where slip may be present, there seems to be no change in grain size or in original composition, but rather there appears to be the effect of bleaching, as the zone of possible slip is much lighter in color than the rest of the specimen. The application of slip is not the only possible explanation for the thin surficial zone.

2.2.4. Botanical Analysis
(N. M. Magalousis and T. Mortenson)

An attempt was made to isolate specific botanical forms embedded within ceramic artifacts from Terqa and Dilbat. Evidence of botanical forms is thus far only visible in outline structure left as the original organic matter oxidized during the firing process.

The attempts of plant identification, and thus localization of specific forms within this geographic region, were frustrated on two points for this preliminary evaluation: (1) the sampling was small (50 samples), and (2) extremely high magnification is required to produce sufficient anatomical/morphological structures to support any taxonomic determination. In a preliminary fashion, organic material appears to be a partially decomposed reed form that is found presently in several regions of the Euphrates. This would indicate that ceramic fabric (wet clay) was obtained from the backwater regions of the Euphrates River, and also that little attempt was made by the ancients to remove this natural tempering material. Modern ceramic manufacturers in Syria seem to acquire clay fabric from similar sources, but go through an elaborate process to remove this organic material, possibly for aesthetic reasons.

2.3. Cultural Analysis Considerations

Based on this initial study, the evidence seems to indicate that the ceramic shards from either Terqa or Dilbat, with the two exceptions noted for Terqa, were made of about the same raw material—both paste and temper—and by potters using essentially the same techniques.

The color differences in the specimens from both Terqa and Dilbat suggest that the conditions of firing or baking may have differed, because of the somewhat different amount or extent of the oxidation of the iron minerals in some specimens versus others. The different colors observed are believed not to have derived from compositional differences so much as from oxidizing versus reducing environments of firing. Future research will attempt to determine specific and defined differences between the Terqa, Mari and Dilbat sampling.

The differences in both the amounts and shapes of the voids or open spaces in the fragments cause some interesting questions to be raised about the methods of making the ceramics. The consistency of the fabric which produced the very porous ceramics must have been significantly more viscous than the fabric which made the specimens with sparse small voids. Perhaps this was by design. Perhaps the more porous, hence lighter (in weight), pots were designed for one purpose, the heavier vessels for another. Or perhaps the less weighty parts served as handles, or possibly as decorations, whereas the heavier less porous and probably more durable material formed the vessel proper. There are a number of other possibilities. The porosity—shapes and sizes of the voids—should be a fertile area for continued study.

A very careful analysis of the kinds, shapes and amounts of minerals forming the temper should be done as part of a continuing study. Particular efforts should be made to identify the less common minerals to learn if differences here might be significant. This initial examination of the "broad brush" type did not disclose what appeared to be significant differences in either the Terqa or Dilbat samples, although these samples compared to ceramics from elsewhere in the world disclose vast differences, in the clay, the paste, in the minerals that composed the temper, in structures in the paste, and to a certain extent differences in the amounts and shapes of the voids in the specimens.

It appears clearly from this initial research that petrographic methods that use the polarizing microscope have a considerable potential for use in reconstructing ancient methods of ceramics manufacture, the kinds of raw material used, and very possibly in tracing the evolution of techniques in ceramics making.

It is recommended that for similar studies:

1. A fragment of the ceramic from which the thin section is made be supplied with the thin section.

2. Care be exercised in thin-section preparation to insure the removal of all extraneous grinding material before cementing procedures are done, to attain an even thickness of the thin section from side to side and end to end, and to avoid gouging the specimen during the grinding process. High-quality thin sections are essential to obtain the desired results.

3. PRELIMINARY ANALYSIS OF TERQA AND DILBAT CERAMICS BY ATOMIC ABSORPTION SPECTROSCOPY

V. Gritton and N. M. Magalousis

3.1. Introduction

3.1.1. Optical Emission
(G. Alexander, L. McAnulty, N. M. Magalousis)

Optical emission analysis was conducted on the artifactual assemblage prior to atomic absorption analysis, for two reasons. First, our intent was to fingerprint or determine what elements were actually contained in the artifacts on an overall basis. Twenty-six elements were tested for by the emission method: P, Na, K, Ca, Mg, Zn, Cu, Fe, Mn, B, Al, Si, Ti, V, Co, Ni, Mo, Cr, Sr, Ba, Li, Ag, Sn, Pd, Be, Cd.[1] The analysis indicated an approximate content of 70-76 percent; the remaining content may have consisted of carbonaceous material.

The second objective was to determine, in a general sense, the concentrations and levels of magnitude of elements; this would provide some insight into the standard ranges needed during atomic absorption analysis.

3.1.2. Atomic Absorption

This portion of the research will concern itself mainly with substantive data relating directly to or affecting the artifactual assemblage, such as sample selection and preparation. A more technical explanation of this portion has been reported in *Archaeological Chemistry II*, 1978.

The theory, technique and application of atomic absorption spectroscopy (AAS) are well known to chemists and are described extensively in the literature, which is estimated at nearly 1,000 papers a year. Excellent sources of information are the Annual Review issues (April) of *Analytical Chemistry* and the *Annual Reports on Analytical Atomic Spectroscopy* from the Society for Analytical Chemistry (London). Several pertinent references are listed in the bibliography.

Two reports directly concerning the application of AAS to ceramics of archaeological interest

---

[1] Instrumentation, Direct Readout Spectrograph made by Applied Research.

serve as a basis for procedural matters. The first of these is Magalousis (1975) and contains the method employed prior to the current study; the second is by Hughes et al. (1976).

The problems associated with AAS may be grouped into four somewhat interrelated areas: (1) sampling and sample preparation; (2) sample decomposition; (3) standards; (4) instrumentation. A brief discussion concerning sampling and instrumentation will be found below.

3.2. Technical Procedures

3.2.1. Sampling and Sample Preparation

3.2.1.1. OBTAINING THE GROSS SAMPLE

It is difficult to make any simple assessment of this problem. In many, if not most, cases a specific technique must be determined on a sample-to-sample basis. If the entire shard cannot be used, the difficulties become compounded.

Several methods of sampling have been proposed. In order of decreasing value, from the point of view of the analyst, are crushing an entire shard; drilling through representative portions; taking a small chip; and abrading a portion of the shard.

The sample obtained is very important—the results of an analysis can be no better than the quality of the sample. If the sample used for analysis is not truly representative of the item under investigation, the results are worse than useless.

A casual examination of the shards currently being studied is enough to reveal that many are visibly nonhomogenous. Layers and striations are easily seen (refer to Thin Section Report 2.1.). If the entire shard is crushed, finely ground and well mixed, then the analytical sample taken will represent the best estimate possible of the composition of the entire object. This is the method utilized in the present study.

3.2.1.2. SAMPLE SIZE

In general, the larger the size of the analytical sample, within reasonable limits, the better. The number of particles which should comprise a sample is a function of both the degree of homogeneity of the sample and the concentration of the material in the sample (Harris and Kratochivil, 1974). Since we are concerned largely with trace elements in materials which may be rather nonhomogenous, a large number of particles is needed. Large samples, however, are more tedious and expensive to work up, so some compromise must be made. The present study employs 0.25 g. samples. This is believed to be adequate. Estimation of particle size by microscopy indicates that portions of this size will provide representative samples.

3.3. Instrumentation and Analysis

Since the AA technique is now well established, the instrumentation is in general of high quality. Still, because it is such a widely used analytical method, each year sees improvements in design, flexibility and ease of use.

The instrument being used in the current study is a Varian/Techtron model 1200. This is a rather compact unit with considerable flexibility and is very convenient to operate. The unit needs very little maintenance or repair, and it takes minimal time to train personnel. More sophisticated units providing automatic background correction would enhance the utility of the method.

3.4. Practical and Conceptual Applications of Atomic Absorption Analysis

The application of atomic absorption analysis in archaeology may be looked upon conceptually and practically. AA is a proven technique; its credibility and sensitivity have for several years been depended upon in the fields of medicine, industry, soil science, and now archaeology. If the analytical circle in archaeology is to be completed, procedures and standards must be followed prior to AA analysis and after, during computer and interpretive phases.

There are good reasons for utilizing atomic absorption instrumentation, as a minimal purchase cost for equipment is necessary, approximately $8,000-18,000 per unit, and a minimal amount of maintenance and repair is required. Also AA saves time, as rapid and direct readout is obtained. This readout may be immediately relayed to existing data storage banks for evaluation, updating and further study.

Archaeologists universally have found funding to be a major consideration in element analysis research. For this reason, AA should be seriously considered, as one may expect to pay as much as $250 per sample using alternate forms of instrumentation such as neutron activation; AA is dramatically below this cost.

Atomic absorption is also flexible and mobile; this mobility allows AA to be established directly in the field or in areas of high archaeological interest. These archaeological regions could establish compact, standardized laboratory units utilizing atomic absorption, as well as other applicable instrumentation. Laboratory expenses could be shared by several archaeological institutes, thus creating international standardization and an even more economical profile than suggested previously. Laboratories of this nature would also alleviate the need of physically transporting artifactual material between international borders, which in the past has proved to be time-consuming, detailed and expensive.

For a detailed explanation of the analytical procedures utilized for this research refer to *Archaeological Chemistry II*, Gritton and Magalousis, 1978.

4. ANALYTICAL FINDINGS BY ATOMIC ABSORPTION ANALYSIS

N. M. Magalousis

4.1. Introduction

A controlled, comprehensive atomic absorption (AA) study has been initiated, a type of study which may be viewed as a foundation for further long-ranged and detailed analyses of this type. The research has been successful in streamlining several aspects of sample acquisition and preparation for AA testing. This simplifies or formalizes primary stages of this type of analysis which in turn may make the process more convenient and acceptable for laboratories to utilize in an international sense. Only small notations of the streamlining process have been reported in this paper; the entire process will be published at a later date.

4.2. Assemblage and Elements Analyzed

The artifactual assemblage of interest under investigation consisted of bricks from Terqa, ceramics from Terqa, Dilbat and Mari, and soils from Terqa. Terqa and Mari are located in the northern Mesopotamian region, Dilbat in the southern portion (refer to General Map).

In this phase of atomic absorption analysis we concentrated on the elements of Fe, Co, Cu, Ni, Mn, Cr, Pb, Ag, Cd, K, Zn and Na.[2] Generalized patterns began to appear during this phase, although the data is not yet conclusive.

4.3. General Trends

Based on the present sampling, a significant difference in chemical composition exists between the northern ceramic samples from Terqa (and Mari) and the southern samples from Dilbat, as noted in graphs.

The Terqa ceramics comparatively indicate high readings in Co, Cr, and Pb , while the Dilbat samples indicate high readings in Cd, Zn, Mn, Ag, Cu, and Ni. This provides indication that *sourcing* is quite possible and will be productive within the Mesopotamian region (samples of interest: Terqa 1-97, Dilbat D1-D15). Practically, this brightens the possibilities of reconstructing ancient trade, political and social associations throughout the region if research projects in the future are coordinated and systematized with one another.

4.3.1. Ceramic and Soil Samples

Terqa ceramics and soil concentrations correspond closely to one another and, in a general sense, with other samples from northern Mesopotamia, with the exception of Baghouz, which does not compare closely to either northern or southern samples.

Mari ceramics and soils are similar to Terqa samples, although the Mari concentrations are far less scattered and have a more defined configuration.

4.3.2. Brick Samples

Four brick samples (A,B,C,D) from Terqa were analyzed and their concentrations correspond to Terqa ceramics and soils; these same samples do not closely correspond with any other samples. If it is determined through further analysis that building construction materials from on-site sources relate well to ceramics and soils (taking into account tempers and additives), we may, through the use of building materials, isolate a fingerprint profile of almost all archaeological sites. This concept would solve many analytical problems that presently exist in the area of element analysis. If analysts were to depend on this concept for fingerprinting, a formal corpus of building materials would have to be formulated for all archaeological sites.

4.4. Prospects for the Future

Additional research is necessary to define more precisely clustering trends and expand analysis into additional areas of interest and importance to the archaeologist and archaeometrist.

A few aspects of our expanded analysis are as follows:
1. Tests have been made to determine the contamination factors involved in washing ceramics in

---

2 Sample preparation differed between Terqa and Dilbat; refer to Magalousis and Hughes et al. noted in Section 3.1.2.

river water, for example, the Euphrates River, versus distilled and DI water. From preliminary analyses, there are strong indications that contamination does occur; this is indicated by higher concentrations of Ca, Mg, K, and Na. An additional contamination test is being conducted to determine if gypsum used in ancient and modern periods to create a cementing agent between building bricks significantly affects the chemical composition of the bricks. If there is a significant effect, our views on utilizing local building construction materials as a basis for chemical fingerprinting of local wares may be altered.

2. Concerning trade, it is important to the archaeologist to identify the contents of various vessels, including burial urns, in an attempt to identify offerings. This is not always an easy task, as decomposition may have reached advanced stages. In this area of interest, atomic absorption may be able to assist in the identification of substances if we first concentrate our analysis on known materials of ancient and modern vintage. This concept is clearly within the range of possibility and could prove highly productive in the support and substantiation of data acquired through standard corporal classification and traditional chemical analysis of the artifactual assemblage.

3. Computer processing of data for this type of analysis on an international basis has not yet been established. Our intent is to perfect more fully the multivariant computer concepts advanced by Dr. G. Miller and the late Dr. D. Bunker from the University of California at Irvine. These generalized concepts have been noted in the Appendix of this paper.

As noted previously, several of our research objectives are in formative or preliminary phases. This formative status allows our research to be somewhat flexible and interdisciplinary in nature. Conceptually, a well organized and synchronic interdisciplinary effort by a variety of researchers is the most promising means of extracting useful data from archaeological materials. It would be most beneficial to archaeologists and archaeometrists to seriously formulate standards and goals for this research effort on an international basis and establish interdisciplinary and international laboratories in key locations, in order to conduct a large portion of this research.

5. CONCLUSIONS

5.1. Terqa Ceramics

Mineral compositions of temper in Terqa specimens consist mostly of quartz, orthoclase and plagioclase, with lesser amounts of augite, hornblende and some unidentified small secondary minerals. Temper fragments range in size from silt size to as much as 1.0 mm. in maximum diameter. A number of samples contain as little as 2 percent transparent temper materials, while others have more than 22 to 23 percent (Samples T-28 and T-43).

Except for the difference in the amount of temper, there seems to be little to distinguish one sample from another. Two specimens, however, are distinctly different; their temper includes relatively large (1.0 mm. or more in diameter) round grains of olivine or augite, intergrown with lath-shaped plagioclase minerals. These samples were manufactured from distinctly different raw materials (T-22 and T-45).

The most distinguishing feature of the paste is the color, which ranges from a light olive green to a red-brown. Between these two extremes are reddish-gray and reddish-brown hues, the amount of oxidation apparently giving a weak to strong reddish cast to the samples.

Voids (holes) in these specimens range from 10 percent to 50 percent. The size and shape of the voids may represent temperature and various tempers. Samples ranging from 45 to 50 percent are

T-10 and T-14; most samples are within a 10 to 23 percent range. In specimens with less than 10 percent voids, the open spaces are commonly rounded.

Several samples appear to be slipped, although they are not slipped. The area that appears to be slipped is probably due to the firing process. Thickness of this area is 0.3 to 0.7 mm. (Samples T-37 and T-44).

5.2. Dilbat Ceramics

Temper is composed of opaque and transparent minerals, magnetite, hematite and ilmenite, ranging in amount from one to 10 percent of the total sample.

Most of the transparent minerals consist of quartz, orthoclase and plagioclase, as well as augite and olivine. Few samples contain temper in amounts greater than 10 percent.

Paste is fine grained, less than 0.08 mm. in size, and coloration ranges from olive-green, reddish-brown, gray-brown, to nearly black.

Voids in the ceramics range from 20 to 50 percent of the total sample. Large voids range from 1.2 to 2 mm. in dimension and tend to be elongated; small voids tend to be rounded (Sample D-2-10).

One or two samples contain a slip (D-3-5), other samples did not even suggest a slip.

5.3. Cultural Considerations

Ceramics from both Terqa and Dilbat seem to be similar in technique of manufacture and general raw material composition, with the exceptions previously noted. Firing techniques may have been somewhat different between the two sites, noted by the varying extent of oxidation and coloration.

The difference in shape and amount of voids cause interesting questions about technique of manufacture and type of temper.

5.4. Botanical Analysis

Our present botanical analysis did not meet with a great deal of substantive success as our sampling was small.

In the future, botanical analysis may have a great deal of potential in sourcing ceramics artifacts derived from isolated or special locations. Advances in this area of study must be preceded by floral identification of most drainage areas adjacent to the Mesopotamian area. Another step must follow, a detailed microscan analysis of ceramics containing botanical samples, in an attempt to identify certain species.

5.5. Optical Emission and Atomic Absorption

Optical emission analysis was conducted mainly for two purposes: 1) to determine what elements actually were contained within the ceramic artifacts and 2) to determine the relative concentrations. Atomic absorption analysis was used to determine more precise quantitative concentrations.

This analysis revealed a comparatively high percentage of potassium in soils, clays and bricks. This could be due to various organic materials found in clay sources; this may indicate that the sources were located near the site, in backwater riverine regions that would be used as watering areas for livestock (*Science,* Vol. 197, September 30, 1977, Number 4311).

5.6. Atomic Absorption Conclusions

Atomic Absorption (AA) has in this research proven to be comparatively inexpensive and convenient in the analysis of soils and ceramics. Practically and conceptually, AA has the capability of becoming a significant analytical instrument in archaeology based on its flexibility, mobility, accuracy and inexpensive nature.

In addition, international atomic absorption laboratories may be located in areas of high archaeological activity. These laboratories may be utilized by several institutes of archaeology; this in turn would provide centralized and more standardized analytical procedures concerning element analysis of artifactual data. Also, technical, methodological and interpretive goal orientations would become more clear on an international basis.

The analysis discussed in this paper concentrated on the elements Fe, Co, Cu, Ni, Mn, Cr, Pb, Ag, Cd, K, Zn, N2. At this point only generalized patterns or trends have been determinable between ceramics and soils from Terqa and Dilbat.

Based on our sampling, several interesting trends have appeared: 1) There seemed to be a distinct element concentration difference between ceramic samples from Terqa and samples from Dilbat. 2) Element concentrations indicate comparatively high quantities of Co, Cr and Pd in the Terqa samples while Cd, Zn, Ag, Cu, Ni were high in the Dilbat samples. This type of data strongly indicate that sourcing can be applied to the Mesopotamian area and will gain in validity as more chemical and geologic data are systematically acquired (refer to Element Concentration Chart, Samples T-1 through T-97 and D-1-1 through D-15-8).

It is hoped that with mapping and charting element concentrations within the Mesopotamian area a firmer insight may be acquired concerning the flow of trade and political associations during Ancient History.

Two interesting spinoff projects have evolved from the original chemical research: 1) In some cases, it may be feasible to determine indigenous element clay profiles from building materials; this data may then be compared to the presumed local and traded ceramics, and 2) the recently proposed computer concepts by Dr. D. Bunker and Dr. G. Miller, University of California at Irvine. These concepts center on a more active interaction between the operator and the actual computer analysis; that is, the user actually talks to the program and makes decisions as calculation proceeds. This allows the user to nucleate and evaluate situations as they arise.

APPENDIX I

PROPOSED PATTERNING PROCEDURE FOR MULTI-ELEMENT AND MULTI-VARIABLE CHEMICAL ANALYSIS

G. Miller

A modern approach to Archeometry demands that considerable effort be made to examine the scientific data acquired through chemical and other analytical methods for relationships that exist between the sampling of objects (artifacts) and raw materials. These relationships may exist because of a common source of material origin or of processing. However, since naturally related materials are generally not highly homogenous and are often subject to chemical change as a result of subsequent geological and historical events either before or after the material is utilized by man, the distinction of relatedness between different samples is not always obvious. Some form of technical assistance to the judgment of the "sorter" is necessary, particularly if large amounts of information are available, such as the case with multielemental chemical analysis.

Several forms of computer programs have been developed to attempt to handle such a multidimensional sorting problem. Such routines are often entitled "clustering" or "pattern recognition" since they aim to provide an output that indicates the relatedness of certain members of the sample set to each other. Many such routines suffer from the drawback, however, that in spite of caution on the part of the operator, certain outputs become "forced" either by the order in which the data are input, or by the scaling applied or by the existence of occasional missing data points. In addition, since the "pattern" criteria are, to a considerable extent, preset, the computer makes the final judgment rather than the operator!

For assistance and test purposes in this study, we intend to use a new method developed by the late Professor Don Bunker, University of California at Irvine, which shows considerable promise for providing true data in examining the relatedness of a group of samples.

This program is more properly called a facilitator than a recognizer, since it does not attempt to replace the human judgment of the archaeologist or conservator, but assists their judgment in forming clusters. All such programs treat analyses, stylistic points, and other attributes as components in a vector space. The common measure of relatedness is Euclidean—$[\Sigma(x_i-y_i)^2]^{1/2}$—or Mahalanobis—$[\Sigma(x_i-y_i)^p]^{1/p}$— distance. Data, in logarithmic form in the case of elemental analyses, is usually first scaled to zero mean and unit Gaussian dispersion.

Our technique differs as follows. In place of Euclidean distance we use the inner product $(\Sigma_i x_i y_i)$ and in place of Mahalanobis measure we use a variably angular—or radial—separation enhancing formula $x_i y_i \cos \alpha / <x_i y_i>$, $\cos \alpha = \Sigma_i x_i y_i / x_i y_i$. The distribution of mean component value for n-dimensional random vectors is as $2(n-1)^{-1}$ rather than as derived from Gaussian, and this is how we scale to unit dispersion. (Forcing a Gaussian, a bad habit of statisticians, produces a distribution intermediate between what we use and random "orthant"/ —generalized quadrant—sampling, but much nearer to the latter as dimensionality increases.)

The primary advantage of all this is that inner product measure has a natural zero of unrelatedness: $\Sigma \chi_i y_i = 0$, orthogonality, approached by random vector pairs as dimensionality grows large. Thus it is impossible to form spurious superclusters, as happens if distance-type relatedness criteria are made too large. Secondary advantages are that missing analyses may be set to zero, corresponding merely to projection on a smaller number of dimensions, with maximal preservation of relatedness; and that stylistic and analytical data may be freely mixed.

The program in interactive, that is, the user "talks" to it and makes decisions as the calculation proceeds. Specific objects may be used to nucleate groups, or the key element may be found by maximization of combined relatedness. At this junction the operator makes a decision, as contrasted with conventional programs in which there is recourse to complicated statistical procedures (k-nearest neighbor, discriminant, and so on). Bunker's view was that if the separation is not apparent to the eye with this measure, it will be a precarious one by other methods. Radial/angular separation enhancement or systematic suppression of interfering analyses may be invoked whenever the operator feels a need for them.

Studies are under way on techniques for better determining the confidence limits for atomic absorption measurements and for applying these limits on weighting factors in their and other patterning procedures.

APPENDIX II

ARCHAEOLOGICAL REGISTRY, CATALOG AND ANALYSIS FORM
Data should be entered on this form completely and accurately

PART I

Artifact catalog no.	Site Number	Stratigraphic e.g. level	Identification centimeters / date

Map Coordinates	Artifact (e.g. shard)	Body Part (e.g. base, rim)

PART II

1) Where was this form completed:
   University Laboratory __ Field Laboratory __ Field __

2) Light Source: Natural __ Fluorescent __ Incandescent __

3) Has the artifact been cleaned (data for nuclear analysis):
   Water __ River __ Tap __ Ultrasonic __ Unwashed __
   Unknown __   Other _____

4) Has any possible ancient or modern contamination occurred:
   (e.g. bitumen found in a garbage drainage area) Yes __   No __

5) How are samples stored: plastic bag __ plastic vials __
   cloth bags __ paper containers __ other _____

PART III

Munsell Soil Color Chart _____   Give closest numerical
                          date   relationship _____

1) Exterior fabric _____   Luster _____

2) Interior fabric _____   Luster _____

3) Interior body
   fabric (temper) _____   Luster _____

4) Fire scars from: Kiln __ or Utilization __

Wentworth Scale - Size determination of particulation _____

5) Impurities: Type _____   Temper size _____
   Size (exterior) _____   (interior) _____

PART IV

1) <u>Note surface alterations</u>   Incized __ Glazed __
   Wheel marks __ Rope marks __ Other _____

2) <u>Technique of manufacture</u>   Coil __ Wheel __ Pressed (basket) __ Other _____

3) <u>Cultural Type</u> (e.g. Babylonian)_____

4) <u>Condition</u> whole __ complete __ reconstructable __ incomplete __

5) <u>Height</u>_____ Thickness (body)_____ Diameter (rim)_____ (base)_____ (body)_____

6) <u>Fired</u>   Heavily __ Moderately __ Lightly __

7) <u>Photographic Record Number</u> _____

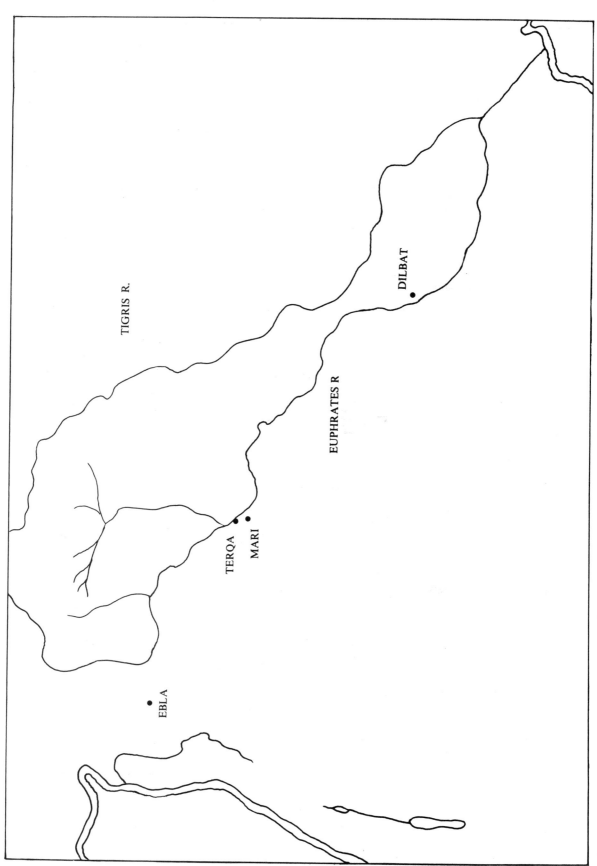

Map 1. Mesopotamia

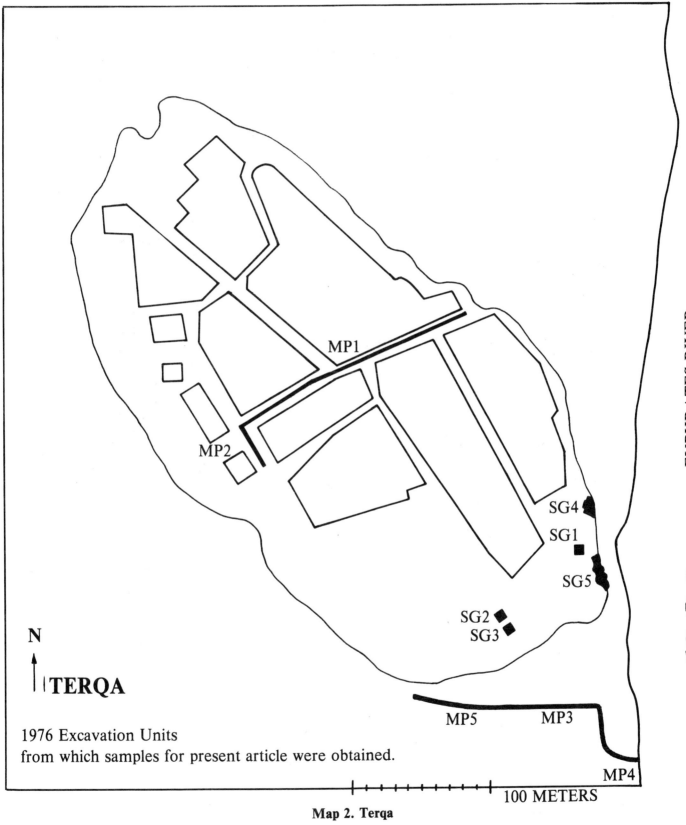

EUPHRATES RIVER

MP1

MP2

SG4

SG1

SG5

SG2

SG3

N

TERQA

1976 Excavation Units
from which samples for present article were obtained.

MP5   MP3

MP4

100 METERS

Map 2. Terqa

GRAPHS

Abbreviations

PROVENIENCE OF SAMPLES		
DC	-	Dilbat Ceramics
TC	-	Terqa Ceramics
TS	-	Terqa Soils
Br	-	Bricks A-D
TBr	-	Other Terqa Bricks
Jar	-	Terqa Burial Jars
Bu	-	Terqa Burials
G1	-	Terqa Gypsum Crystals with Soils
G2	-	Terqa Gypsum Crystals
MC	-	Mari Ceramics
MS	-	Mari Soils
MBr	-	Mari Brick
aE	-	Soil from across Euphrates
BS	-	Bahguz Soil
CMC	-	Ceramic Manufacturing Company (clay)

ELEMENTS	
Ag	silver
Al	aluminum
B	boron
Ba	barium
Be	beryllium
Ca	calcium
Cd	cadmium
Co	cobalt
Cr	chromium
Cu	copper
Fe	iron
K	potassium
Li	lithium
Mg	magnesium
Mn	manganese
Mo	molybdenum
Na	sodium
Ni	nickel
P	phosphorus
Pb	lead
Si	silicon
Sn	tin
Sr	strontium
Ti	titanium
V	vanadium
Zn	zinc

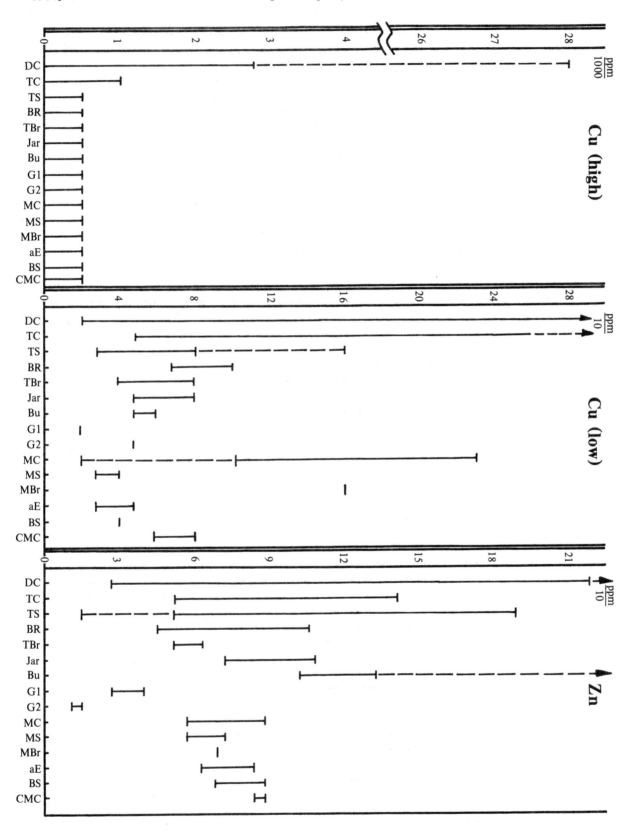

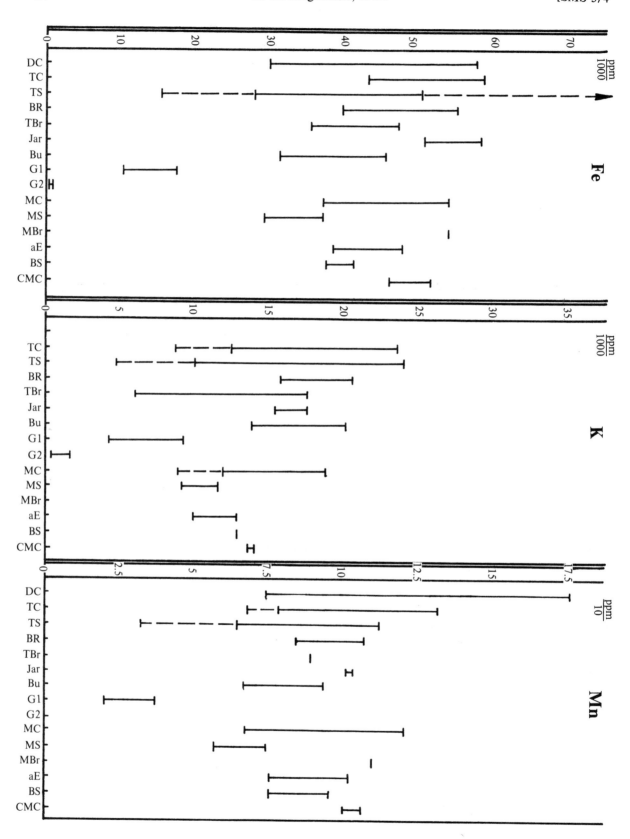

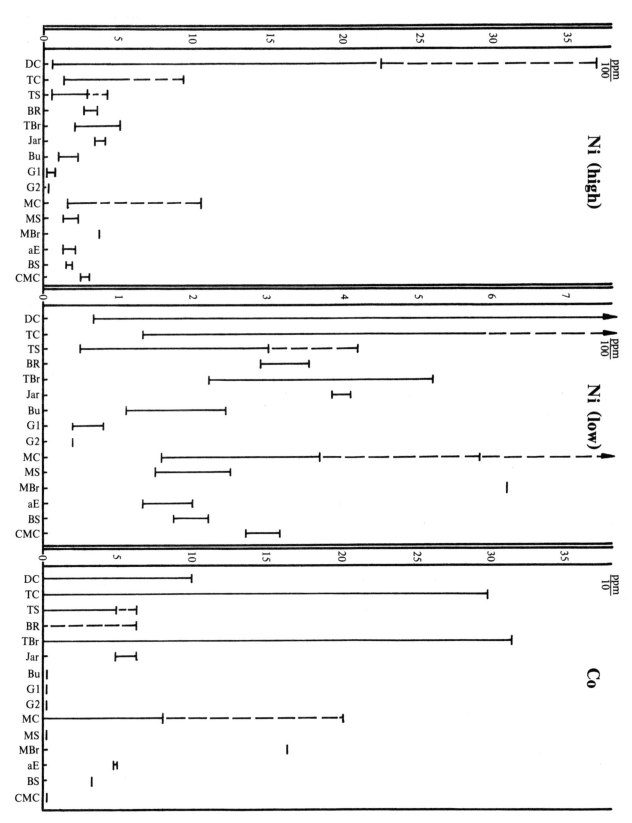

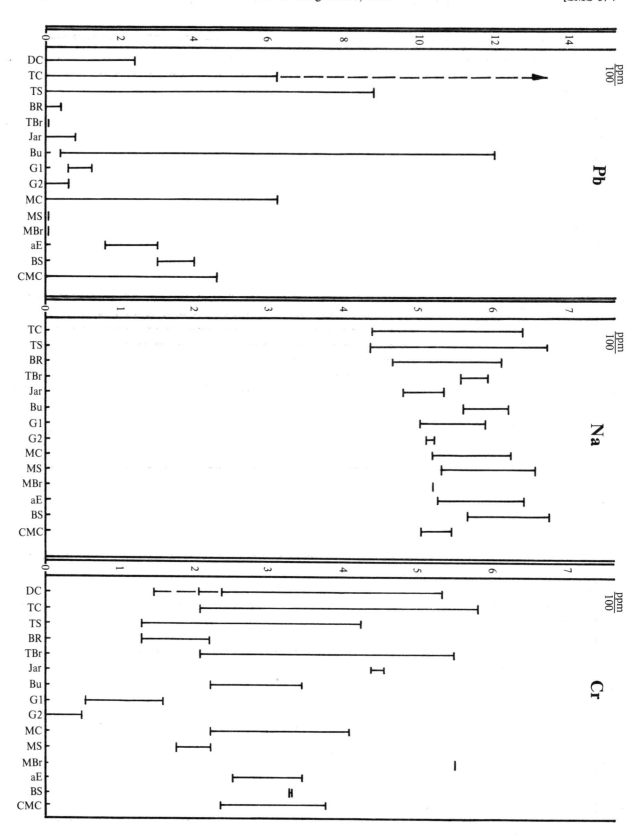

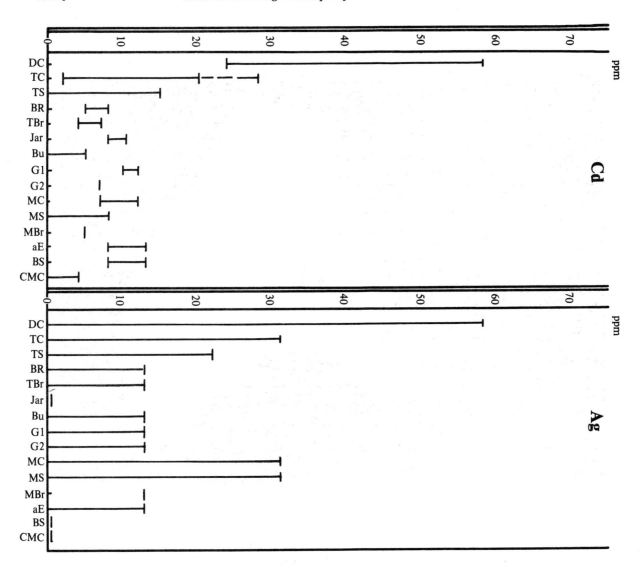

Illustration 1.

Close range photographs of ceramics for the purpose of documentation to accompany catalog forms.

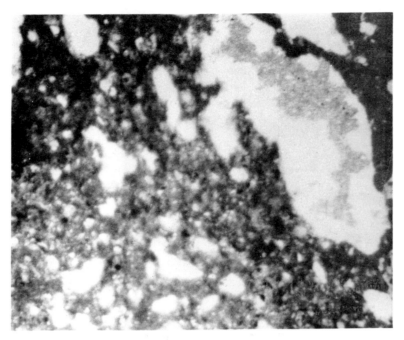

Illustration 2. Sample T-9

Large white areas represent voids or pores in the specimen. The largest void contains finely comminuted crystalling debris produced by the grinding of the thin section. Smaller, sharply defined white areas represent transparent minerals of the temper. Photo by transmitted light, 55X enlargement.

Illustration 3. Sample T-43

Very fine temper minerals grade into silt-size paste fragments without a break in grain size. Only a very few small voids occur in this specimen, which contains the least void space and generally the smallest fragments of any studied. Photo by transmitted light, 55X enlargement.

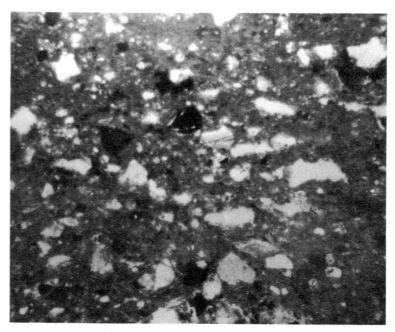

Illustration 4. Sample T-40

Irregular white areas represent voids. Angular, more sharply defined white areas represent transparent minerals, a part of the temper. In this specimen there is a well-defined break in fragment size between the temper and the paste. Photo by transmitted light, 55X enlargement.

Illustration 5. Sample T-45

Only two thin sections (of 88 studied) has the unusual mineral arrangement shown in this photomicrograph. The lath-shaped minerals, some of which show relict albite (plagioclase feldspar) twining, are intergrown with a much altered basic mineral, either olivine or augite, in these small rounded rock fragments that compose much of the temper in the two specimens. Photo by transmitted light, 55X enlargement.

ABBREVIATIONS

AA	atomic absorption
AAS	atomic absorption spectroscopy
C	centigrade
DI	deionized
et al.	and others
g.	gram
g/l	grams per liter
H	Hughes et al. procedure for AA sample preparation
HF	high frequency
M	Magalousis procedure for AA sample preparation
g	microgram
mg	milligram
ml	milliliter
mm	millimeter
ppm	parts per million
SG3	excavation unit at Terqa
SG4	excavation unit at Terqa
TPR	*Terqa Preliminary Reports*
UV	ultraviolet

REFERENCES

Analytical Methods for Flame Spectroscopy. Brisbane, Australia: Varian/Techtron [1972].

Angino, E. E. and Billings, G. R. *Atomic Absorption Spectroscopy in Geology.* New York: Elsivier-Billings, 1967.

Buccellati, G. and Kelly-Buccellati, M., "Terqa Preliminary Reports, 1: General Introduction and the Stratigraphic Record of the first Two Seasons," *Syro-Mesopotamian Studies* 1/3 (1977).

Childe, V. Gordon *What Happened in History.* Harmondsworth: 1954 (1942 ed.), Ch. 5.

Gritton, V. and Magalousis, N. M. "Atomic Absorption Spectroscopy of Archaeological Ceramic Materials." In *Archaeological Chemistry II*, edited by G. F. Carter. Symposium, Division of the History of Chemistry. 174th Meeting of the American Chemical Society, Washington, D.C. American Chemical Society, 1978.

Harris, W. E. and Kratochovil, B. *Analytical Chemistry* 48 (1974): 313.

Hughes, M. J.; Corvell, M. R.; and Craddock, P. T. "Atomic Absorption Techniques in Archaeology," *Archaeometry* 18 (1976): 19.

Magalousis, N. M. "Atomic Absorption Spectrophotometric Analysis of Nabataean, Hellenistic and Roman Ceramics in an Attempt to Reconstruct History" (Master's Dissertation on file, UCLA, 1975).

Magalousis, N. M. "Atomic Absorption Spectrophotometric Analysis of Babylonian Ceramics: A Preliminary Evaluation" (research, Institute of Archaeology, UCLA, 1976).

Magalousis, N. M. "The Advantages of Atomic Absorption Analysis Applied to Archaeological Materials." In *Archeo Physiko 10.* Presented at International Symposium on Archaeometry and Archaeological Prospection. Bonn, Germany: Rheinland-Verlag GmbH Köln in Kommission bei Rudolf Habelt Verlag GmbH, 1978.

Price, W. J. *Analytical Atomic Absorption Spectrometry.* London: Hayden & Sons, 1974.

Rantalla, R.T.T. and Loring, D. H. "Multi-element Analysis of Silicate Rock and Trace Elements by Atomic Absorption Spectroscopy." *Atomic Absorption Newsletter* 14, 1975, p. 117.

Shepard, Anna O. *Ceramics for the Archaeologist.* Washington, D.C.: Carnegie Institution, 1976 (reprint of 1954 ed.).

Slavin, W. *Atomic Absorption Spectroscopy,* New York: Interscience (Wiley), 1968.

Suhr, N. H. and Ingamells, C. O. "Solutions and Technique for Analysis of Silicate." *Analytical Chemistry* 38 (1966): 730.